FOR THOSE WHO READ THIS BOOK TO CHILDREN

Here is a child's introduction to mapmaking, to geography at its best. Because children still feel central to their surroundings, their first geography book should literally start with themselves and their own personal world. Geography here is not built on memory of capitals, rivers, and resources, but on child interest and child action. Not isolated facts but their relationships, which children discern through their own discovery, are important to good learning. Therefore, your warm support of the child's initiative and purpose throughout the *"active* reading" of this book will be especially helpful.

S. C.

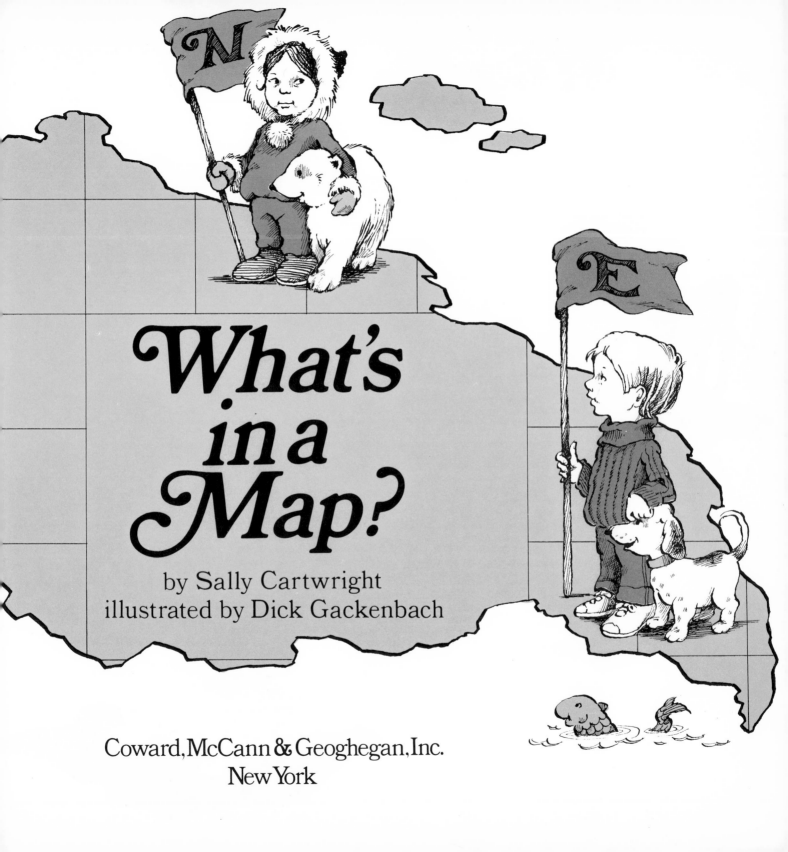

What's in a Map?

by Sally Cartwright
illustrated by Dick Gackenbach

Coward, McCann & Geoghegan, Inc.
New York

General Editor: Margaret Farrington Bartlett

SBN: GB-698-30635-X
SBN: TR-698-20383-6
Second Impression
Library of Congress Cataloging in Publication Data
Cartwright, Sally
What's in a map?
1. Map drawing. 2. Maps—Juvenile literature.
I. Gackenbach, Dick. II. Title.
GA130.C33   912   76-10694
Printed in the United States of America

For City & Country School,
where maps become a child's living tool and
process in one's whole life of learning

A Feeling Map

Wake up in the morning
and lie in bed.
Can you feel your pillow
with your cheek,
with your hands?

Can you find the top and sides
of your long bed?
Can you reach your hands
down each edge
where the sheet
is tucked in?

You are making a feeling map
of your pillow,
of your bed.
Where are *you*
in your feeling map?
How far is your head
from each end of the pillow?
How deeply does your head
sink in the softness?

Slide close to one side
of your bed.
Can you feel the wide space
across the bed to the other side?
Can you feel the warm spot
where you were lying?

Close your eyes.
Feel where your feet are
when you bend your knees.
Feel where your feet are
when you reach your toes
as far down the bed as you can.

It is all part of your feeling map
and knowing where you are in it.

Suppose you open your eyes,
climb out of bed,
and go to the bathroom.
Inside the bathroom
stand by the sink
and close your eyes again.
Feel along the sink.
Find the faucets.
Find the soap.
(Keep your eyes closed!)
Feel the bowl of the sink
and the drain hole.
Close the drain.
Turn on the cold water.

Let it run slowly
until your hand,
pressed flat on the bottom of the bowl,
is just covered with cool water.
Then turn off the water.
If you can do it all
with your eyes closed,
you are making
a feeling map of the sink.

If you have made a good map,
it will stay in your memory safely
for whenever you need it.

You can make feeling maps
of yourself, your bed, your sink.
You can make feeling maps
of your room and your toys.

At school you can
close your eyes
and feel where you are
in a circle of children.
Can you point to each child
and say his or her name
even with your eyes closed?

A feeling map is a good thing to learn.
It is good to feel where you are.
It is good to feel what is around you.

A Paper Map

Try to make a picture map
of yourself in bed.
Then make
a picture map of the sink.
A paper map
is different from
a feeling map.

Paper is thin and flat.
But is the sink flat?
Could it hold water
if it were flat?
Can you show how cold water feels
as it creeps up over your hand?

Here's an interesting thing.
If you draw a tree on paper,
you are not making a real tree.
You are making its *picture*.
If you really want to know a tree,
go see the tree itself.

Walk around it.
How big is it?
Look at its size,
its trunk, its branches.
What does its bark feel like?
Listen to its leaves
if they whisper in the wind.
Pull on the branches
and feel them bend.

A solid, living tree
is very different from a paper picture.
And so it is important
to learn about real things
by your own experience.

It's good to see and feel and hear.
It's good to try things out for yourself.
Like a picture, maps and even words
stand for real things.
They help us tell friends
where we've been
and what we've seen.
It's fun to share

words and maps and pictures
with others.

Now make a paper map of your house.
Go into each room.
See its size.
See where each thing is.

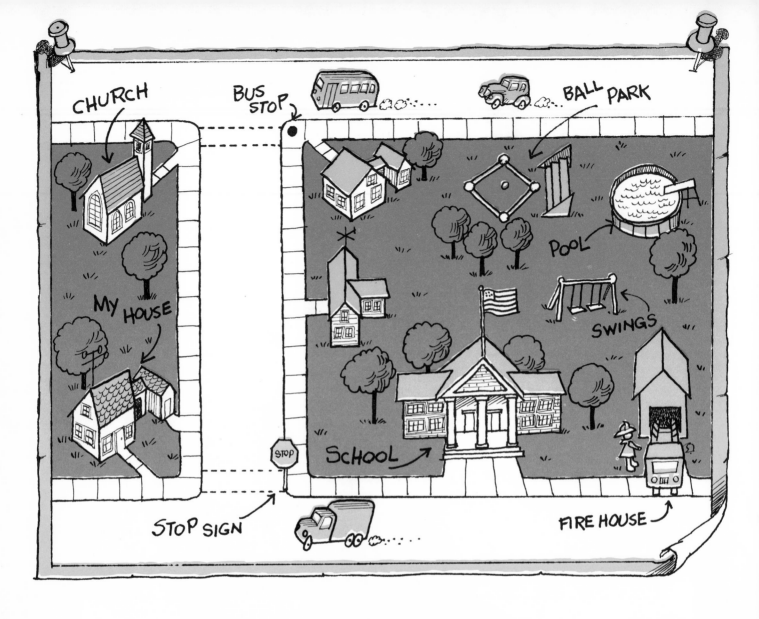

Make a paper map of your street.
Go outside and see where things are.
Start with your house.
What comes next?
What is across the street?

If you take a walk with Mom or Dad,
when you get back home,
can you make a map of where you went?

Can you make a map that shows the way to school?
Can you make a map of your classroom?

Many Ways of Making Maps

We spoke of a feeling map
which you can remember when you like.
Or you can *see* a place
and remember so you'll not forget.
You can make a paper map
with a pencil or with crayons.
You can paint a map on paper, too.
Paper maps help you remember.

You can build a map with blocks.
You need floor space
and blocks to build with.
Try to make a block map of your room
with all its furniture.
Don't forget the door.

25

Make a block map
of your classroom at school.
Make a block map of your house.
Show the different rooms.
Now you can play

with your block house.
Make a block map of your street.
It is good to work with a friend at this.
You can help each other
remember where things are.

When you go on a long walk
or a car trip,
watch for how the road turns.
Watch for hills and fields and woodland.
Watch for streams and rivers and ponds.
You can make maps of where you have been.

You can make a map with sand, too.
It is best if the sand is damp
so that your roads and houses
and hills stay put.

You can poke little sticks in the sand for trees.
You can make a low, smooth, flat place
for a pond.
You can use chips of wood for boats.

Pretend Maps

When you have taken lots of trips
and seen and done lots of things,
you might like to make a pretend map.
Put roads and rivers and lakes
wherever you like.
You can make a country of your own.
But if you want to make your map
so it *could* be a real place,
there is much you need to know
from your own experience—

Why do people build roads?

Why bridges?

Why use ships?

Why have farms and factories?

And why would a town be on a harbor?

ABOUT THE AUTHOR

Sally Cartwright has taught elementary science and geography for many years to children in nursery through grade eight. With a master's degree from Bank Street College of Education and further graduate work at Harvard, Mrs. Cartwright has devoted her professional life to developing effective learning environments with and for children. Each experience in her books has been tested for years by children from her own classrooms and at the Watertown Cooperative Nursery School near Boston, where she was educational director, as well as also put to use in schools where she has been or is educational consultant.

Her writing for teachers has been published here and abroad, and this is her eighth science-related book for children. Her books have received such recognition as an "outstanding science trade book of the year" *(Water Is Wet)*, Junior Literary Guild selection *(Sand)*, and honors from the New York Academy of Sciences *(Sunlight)*.

ABOUT THE ARTIST

Dick Gackenbach grew up in Allentown, Pennsylvania. Upon graduating from high school in 1944, Mr. Gackenbach joined the Navy. After World War II he studied art in Washington, D.C., and then came to New York City to study at the Janeson Franklin School of Art.

Formerly one of the creative directors of the J. C. Penney Company, Mr. Gackenbach left both New York City and advertising to live in the country and embark on a new career in children's books. He has written and illustrated *Claude the Dog, Claude and Pepper, Do You Love Me?,* and *Hattie Rabbit* among others.

Mr. Gackenbach lives on a mountain top near Washington Depot, Connecticut, with his two dachshunds.